# Contents

# The seasons set the tone

**THE NICE THING** about customs and traditions is that they are constantly changing. When no longer of use, they are either forgotten or re-cast in a different mould. They often have ancient roots, and some date as far back as pagan Sweden. Many traditions have been introduced from other countries, for example by German traders or by the Protestant church. Some customs are so old that we have forgotten their origins. But we observe them nevertheless, because we have always done so and because we have come to enjoy them. They have grown to be a part of our life cycle, giving shape to our lives and giving us a sense of time, and also lending the year a seasonal rhythm.

In Sweden, many customs are closely associated with the changing seasons. Swedes celebrate summer with an intensity that can only be found in a people who have just endured a long, dark winter. They light candles at Advent and pay homage to a white-clad Lucia with a crown of candles in her hair. Swedish food tends to be influenced by the seasons. The way it is spiced and cooked often reflects the storage needs of the peasant communities of old, as in the case of pickled herring, freshly salted or smoked meat, or dairy products that have been curdled, boiled or left to mature. Several of Sweden's traditional festivities are linked to the farming year – to spring till age, to the hunting and fishing season or to harvest time. As noted above, however, their original significance may have been lost in the mists of time and replaced by some other import.

It is not simply about the passage of time and human forgetfulness, however. The Swedes are split in their image of themselves: while they are proud of their own history they also become uncomfortable when confronted with that which is deemed continental and internationally acceptable.

When the opportunity arose, Sweden flung itself headlong into the modern era. Its remote position on the map, its remarkable capacity for staying out of wars and its endless supply of timber and ore made Sweden both a rich country and an unusual one by international standards. While other countries experienced conflicts and class divisions, Swedish citizens enjoyed a consensus of opinion and a belief in the future. At times, belief in innovation, in the welfare society – what came to be known as the *folkhem* in Sweden – and in growth was so strong that the country forgot its history. Old customs and traditions were suddenly thought useless. Young people closed their ears to the stories of their elders and refused to look back. The future was waiting just over the horizon and it was simply a matter of getting there as quickly as possible.

In the post-war decades, Swedish society grew

*No summer is complete
without strawberry cake.*

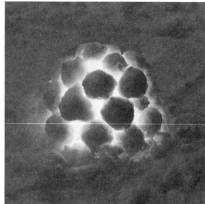

*Freedom at last! School leavers in their white student caps celebrate with friends and family.*

and expanded at record speed. From having been an agrarian nation in the European margins, Sweden climbed to the top of the growth table. New communities developed, roads were widened and the countryside was opened up. Concrete buildings mushroomed everywhere.

Sweden gained prosperity but lost touch with its history. It has taken a long time for Swedes to re-store a balance. In modern Sweden, the old and the new live side by side, sometimes in the form of two parallel narratives, sometimes – but less often – as an integrated whole. The same could be said of all that comes into the country from other parts of the world: people, trends and modes of expression from other cultures and spheres.

Immigration has brought with it new customs and traditions that in time will become woven into the fabric of what we call Swedish society. By the same token, the 'New Swedes' take up old Swedish traditions, and it is often the children who intro-duce them into the family. Daycare centres and schools exert a considerable influence in the social sphere. The result – at best – is cultural cross-fertilisation. Most Swedes already know what the

Muslim month of fasting, Ramadan, involves. Several new traditions have found their way into Swedish life in recent years, usually via the media or as a result of commercial pressures. Valentine's Day and Halloween have now become a feature of the Swedish calendar as well, albeit with some modifications.

A few generations from now, the origins of these customs may have been forgotten, for as soon as a people absorb something in the form of a custom, where it actually originated becomes a matter of little interest. The Swedish Santa Claus is German, but many Swedes believe in him all the same. Lucia was a Sicilian saint, and St Martin's Day takes its name from a French bishop. This does not make any of them less enjoyable.

Most traditional customs are celebrated in the home, with the family. The only real exception is Midsummer, when Swedes, regardless of the weather, want to be outdoors, to meet others and to greet the arrival of summer. But then Midsummer is an occasion with pagan roots. The Lutheran church was not particularly fond of communal festivities and processions, and Sweden's scattered population in combination with the chilly climate meant that celebrations were moved indoors and became a family affair. Times change, however. Visitors to Sweden in wintertime may find the streets deserted, but summer visitors encounter a completely different scene. A wide range of festivals and street parties have become a feature of the Swedish summer in recent years, bringing people together to listen to music, eat and enjoy one another's company.

Numerous 'fiddlers' meets' are held around the country in summertime, focusing in particular on Swedish folk music. The violin or fiddle arrived in Sweden in the 18th century and quickly spread among the peasantry. Indigenous folk music, which is often in triple time, was usually played by a lone fiddler at dances. This musical culture has survived, and the summer meets often attract large numbers of visitors.

The Swedish summer is also a time when many couples marry, as the weather allows them to travel to church in an open pony-and-trap or to wed in a simple ceremony on a rock in the archipelago. Church weddings are still the most popular type of marriage ceremony, despite the fact that the Church of Sweden – which was 'wed' to the State until very recently – is losing both members and visitors. Most people also prefer to hold funeral ceremonies in church.

Christening ceremonies are still a feature of contemporary life in Sweden – again, mostly in summertime – although naming ceremonies of a more homespun character are becoming increasingly popular. Confirmation in the Church of Sweden is still prevalent, but nowadays usually in the form of a summer camp where bible studies are combined with social and other activities.

The elderly sometimes mutter about a loss of values when young people go their own way. Marriage, christenings and confirmation in church used to be rites of passage en route to adulthood and a place in the community. Nowadays, most people do as they please. Swedes are like most others: the street scene is becoming increasingly continental, and manners and customs increasingly international. If you are invited for dinner with a Swedish family today, there is little etiquette to breach. Just remember to say thank you – *tack*! Swedes do it all the time. It's like the English 'please' and 'thank you' rolled into one:

"Could you pass the salt, please (*Kan du skicka saltet, tack*)?"

"Here you are (*Varsågod*)."

"Thank you (*Tack*)!"

# New Year's Eve

**THE SWEDISH NEW YEAR** often coincides with a bout of ice-cold weather. Temperatures, which tend to hover frustratingly around freezing point over Christmas, at least in the south, gradually drop, and by midnight you can see shivering Swedes, up to their knees in heavy snow, toasting one another in champagne and firing off rockets.

It is quite an endearing sight, and it is also symptomatic of modern Sweden. In many respects, Swedes have begun to absorb the continental lifestyle, but somewhere along the way a collision always occurs. In this case, with the climate.

After celebrating Christmas with their immediate families, old or new, and with relatives and those that have married into the family, Swedes like to spend New Year's Eve with their friends.

They don't mind Christmas celebrations being an old-fashioned family affair, but New Year is nowadays supposed to be lavish, ostentatious, international and modern. In city market-halls and delicatessens, last-minute customers fight over the last lobsters and the last box of oysters. At home in the kitchen, people reduce their sauces, caramelise their orange peel and lay the table with the finest dinnerware, tablecloths and candlesticks. They dress up in newly-bought clothes and pretend the icy wind howling outside the door is not there. Tights and high-heeled

Countless rockets light up the
night sky as midnight arrives.

shoes, however, aren't much fun in the grip of midwinter.

During dinner, you discuss both the past year and the year to come. You promise to become a much better person in future, and when the clocks strike midnight you make a New Year's resolution – in Sweden as elsewhere. Many promise to stop smoking, or to lose weight, or to start exercising at a gym or make more money. As a rule, these promises are kept – for a few weeks, at least.

Like many other festive occasions in Sweden, the New Year has become increasingly dominated by the traditional offerings of the media. Each year ends with a live broadcast from the Skansen open-air museum in Stockholm, where the bells chime and a New Year verse (interestingly enough by the English poet Tennyson) is solemnly declaimed to the nation. There's something nice and secure about rounding off the year in front of the TV in your living room.

Many, however, prefer the cold night air. Those who are not lucky enough to live in a town flat with a view tend to seek out public places at midnight from where they can fire off rockets and sneak a look at other people's firework displays. You stand there, enveloped in your heavy winter coat, gazing open-mouthed as the horizon – whether high-rise buildings in silhouette or a sparse line of pine-trees – comes alight, flashing and crackling.

# New Year's Eve

In accordance with the Roman Calendar, the Swedish New Year begins on 1 January. In preindustrial society, it was a part of the Christmastime celebrations. In contrast to Christmas, however, it was mainly a festive occasion for young people. They saw in the year with food, drink and merriment. To mark the transition, and to see off the old year, they fired guns or yelled and screamed, or kicked up a row in some other way.

The turn of the year was considered a magical time, when people tried to foresee the future. One way of telling your future was to mould lead in water and then interpret the figures this produced. Another was to toss shoes. If your shoe landed with the toe pointing towards the door, it meant you would move away or even die during the year.

New Year's Day was thought to betoken the year as a whole. So it was important not to carry anything out of the house, as this meant discarding happiness for the rest of the year. If the sun shone on New Year's Day, a good year could be expected.

Ever since 1893, when the custom began at the Skansen open-air museum in Stockholm, the country's churches have rung in the New Year at midnight.

*'Skål' for the New Year!*

# Valentine's Day

**THE SWEDES' TRADITIONAL** inability to absorb foreign expressions was due not so much to national pride as to a sort of social immobility, coupled at times with a degree of (let's face it!) self-conceit. As time has passed, however, many walls have been torn down, and the most noticeable change to have occurred must surely be that Swedes have become more open to newfangled commercial ideas. Valentine's Day is now a Swedish affair as well, despite having no link whatsoever to the country's past. Back in the 1960s, flower-sellers in Sweden – inspired by their American counterparts – began to launch campaigns promoting Valentine's Day. By the 1980s, the custom had become all-pervasive, and today huge amounts of roses, jelly hearts and pastries are sold as well. The young in particular have adopted the custom.

The idea behind it, though, is praiseworthy – to show your love and appreciation of another. If it happens to boost the country's economy as well, it makes the Swedes even happier.

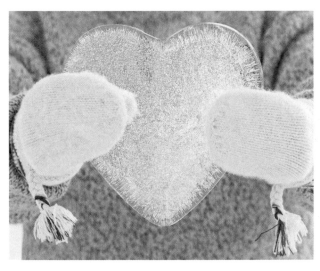

## Valentine's Day

Valentine's Day – which the Swedes call the 'Day of All Hearts' (*Alla hjärtans dag*) – commemorates a Roman martyr. From the Middle Ages, it was celebrated on 14 February in England, Scotland and France by pairing off unmarried young men and women who were to be partners at the coming summer festivities (in Sweden this was done at Whitsun).

During the Middle Ages, young men would compose rhyming love letters to the young women of their fancy, known as Valentine poetry. In the 19th century, the practice was to send printed and illustrated Valentine cards. The custom spread to the US, where young people sent each other heart-shaped cards and/or expensive presents on Valentine's Day.

This custom has since found its way to Sweden, where it became established in the 1980s, principally among young children and teenagers.

*The semla bun-eating tradition tends to begin earlier each year, just like Christmas.*

## Semla

The *semla*, also known as *fettisdags-bulle* or *hetvägg* (from the German heisse Wecken), was originally a wedge-shaped bun that was boiled and eaten hot, first at Shrovetide and later on Tuesdays in Lent. In the 19th century, people started scooping out the middle and filling the bun with marzipan, butter or cream. Later still, a layer of whipped cream was added in the middle. The bun was eaten with hot milk, sugar and cinnamon, but gradually came to resemble a regular cream bun rather than the meal it had previously constituted. Nowadays, pastry shops start selling the buns before Christmas!

# Easter

**SWEDEN IS A LARGE** country with a lengthy coastline, as the tourist brochures keep telling us. So when the big seasonal holidays come round, Swedes embark on long journeys to visit friends and relatives. For although contemporary Swedes are an urban people, most of whom live in cities or large towns, the vast majority still have one foot in the countryside. If they don't have any family left in rural parts, they often possess a holiday cottage there. An agrarian strain runs through Sweden's self-image: this is a nation of strong, sinewy peasants, raised on meat and a lot of turnips.

Most people are agreed that festive occasions in Sweden should be celebrated in the countryside. Easter is no exception.

Easter is the first extended weekend of the spring, and for many this means the first trip out to their holiday cottage, which has been locked and deserted all winter. There are window shutters to be opened and stuffy rooms to be aired. The wood-stoves are lit, and the smoke fills the kitchen, naturally. Coughing and spluttering, you flee out to the

*At Easter, gaily feathered twigs abound both indoors and outdoors.*

*Little Easter witches go hunting for sweets.*

yard, where the wagtails – if you live in southern Sweden, that is – have just begun their mating ritual and the last of the snowdrifts are melting in the pale spring sunshine. In the north, Easter is more of a skiing holiday.

Once the cottage has been cleaned, swept and warmed up, Easter can begin. The members of the family arrive from near and far. At Easter, the aim is to gather as many relatives together as possible.

While in other countries Easter is specifically a religious holiday, it has become a secular one in Sweden. The Swedes are well down in the statistics when it comes to church visits per year, and even if Easter swells the numbers slightly, most people celebrate it at home with their families and relatives. Many of the practices associated with Easter have religious origins, but this is not something that bothers Swedes much. They eat eggs because they have always done so – not because they have just completed a fast. Nowadays, eggs are a favourite accompaniment to the dish of pickled herring that is the centrepiece of most Swedes' Easter meals.

And few associate the omnipresent birch twigs – nowadays decorated with brightly coloured feathers – with the suffering of Christ.

Easter has its own rituals. Children dress up as Easter witches; clad in discarded clothes, gaily coloured headscarves and red-painted cheeks, they go from house to house in the neighbourhood and present the occupants with paintings and drawings in the hope of getting sweets in return. Having consumed all these sweets, they are then given Easter eggs filled with yet more. Parents of a more ambitious turn of mind let the children search for the eggs themselves in a treasure hunt – following clues and solving riddles until they find their prizes.

A traditional Easter lunch is likely to consist of different varieties of pickled herring, cured salmon and Jansson's Temptation (potato, onion and pickled sprats baked in cream). The table is often laid like a traditional smörgåsbord. Spiced schnapps is also a feature of the Easter table. At dinner, people eat roast lamb with potatoes au gratin and asparagus or some other suitable side dish.

*Pickled herring and egg are a popular dish at Easter as well.*

# Easter

In Sweden, the Easter celebrations used to begin with the three days of Shrovetide, full of carnivals, games and revelry. One of the more popular activities was to playfully thrash each other with birch twigs on Shrove Tuesday. Another Shrovetide practice was to toboggan down steep slopes so that the flax would grow tall. People were also supposed to mark Shrove Tuesday by eating seven hearty meals. A 40-day fast then followed, with its own rules concerning food, such as a ban on eating meat or eggs.

Easter, the most important Christian festival of all, commemorates the resurrection of Christ. It begins on Palm Sunday in celebration of his triumphant entry into Jerusalem. In olden times the red-letter days in Holy Week before Easter were governed by church decree. On Maundy Thursday, you were not allowed to spin or chop wood, as this might add to Christ's suffering. Also on that day, witches flew off to consort with the Devil at Mount Blåkulla, and people used to protect themselves by painting crosses on their front doors and hiding broomsticks and rakes so that the witches could not fly on them. Good Friday was spent in quiet contemplation. People dressed in black and ate salty food without anything to drink. Young people thrashed each other with birch twigs. The whole week was designed to recall Christ's suffering and death on the cross.

On Easter Saturday, the celebrations turned joyful, and people began eating eggs again. Eggs were sometimes painted in different colours, probably because they were often given away as presents. In the 19th century, Swedes began filling paper eggs with sweets. In western Sweden, the practice was to light bonfires (still widespread today), fire shotguns and shout to scare away witches. People sent one another anonymous Easter letters with their own designs. The custom of bringing birch twigs into the house and decorating them with coloured feathers dates back to the 1880s. In southern Sweden, egg games, such as eggbashing, have long been popular. Trick-or-treat became an Eastertime tradition in the 19th century, originally practised by adults in masks and costumes, but later by young girls.

# Walpurgis Eve and 1 May

**YOU CAN COLLECT** a whole load of junk in the course of a year. And (in Sweden) much of it ends up on the Walpurgis bonfire – old doors and fencing, branches from pruned fruit trees, discarded bushes and old cardboard boxes. The bonfires are lit all over the country on 30 April.

For students, Walpurgis Eve is a foretaste of summer. Exams are soon over and only a few lectures remain before term ends. On the last day of April, the students don their characteristic white caps and sing songs of welcome to spring, to the budding greenery and to a brighter future.

Choral singing is a popular pastime in Sweden, and on Walpurgis Eve virtually every choir in the country is busy. In every village and neighbourhood, bonfires are lit at dusk, and everyone has experienced that rosy red glow in your face from the heat of the fire and the freezing cold at your back. The nights are still chilly...

A dish to warm you up at a time like this is nettle soup. Nettles are, of course, a weed. They quickly appear when the snow melts, contain large amounts of iron and are best when young and fresh.

Walpurgis celebrations are not a family occasion but rather a public event, and local groups often take responsibility for organising them to encourage community spirit in the village or neighbourhood.

Once the fire dies, many people move on to pubs and restaurants or to friends' parties. The fact that Walpurgis Eve is followed by 1 May – a public holiday in Sweden since 1939 – means that people are not afraid of partying into the night. Those who wish to can sleep throughout the following day, while others mark this traditional workers' day of leave by joining one or other of the May Day marches that parade through the streets of their town or village, beneath banners carrying slogans of a classical or more topical nature.

*Many people celebrate spring with Walpurgis fireworks, then join a May Day march the day after.*

*Choral singers are much in demand at this time of year.*

## Walpurgis Eve

In the Middle Ages, the administrative year ended on 30 April. Accordingly, this was a day of festivity among the merchants and craftsmen of the town, with trick-or-treat, dancing and singing in preparation for the forthcoming celebration of spring. Among farmers and peasants, it was an important day in the calendar as the annual village meeting was held, with eggs and schnapps as refreshments. The meeting also chose a new alderman. At Walpurgis (*Valborg*), farm animals were let out to graze, and ever since the early 18th century bonfires (*majbrasor, kasar* ) have been lit to scare away predators. People also fired guns, shook cowbells or yelled and screamed to keep the predators at bay. In some parts of the country, young people went round singing May songs in return for gifts of food on Walpurgis Eve. Those who gave them nothing were treated to a 'nasty' ditty. Elsewhere, people visited spas to drink the healthgiving water and to amuse themselves.

In town, the bonfires are lit to warm the soul, in the country-side to burn winter refuse.

# National Day

SWEDEN HAS NOT taken part in any of the wars of the modern era, which may explain the Swedes' somewhat guarded attitude towards celebrating a national day. They are proud of their country but don't seem to feel any great need to show it. Previously, 6 June was not a public holiday, and for many people the only sign that this was a special occasion was the decoration of buses with Swedish flags. Every year, the King and Queen take part in a ceremony at Skansen, Stockholm's open-air museum, where the yellow and-blue Swedish flag is run up the mast, and children in traditional peasant costume present the royal couple with bouquets of summer flowers. These days, special ceremonies welcoming new Swedish citizens are held around the country on National Day.

The last time people in general took an active interest in Sweden as a nation-state was at the turn of the last century, when national-romantic winds were blowing through the country and folklore societies and local history museums were established. It was then that 6 June first became a day of celebration. In 2004, the Swedish Riksdag voted to make it a public holiday, which may cause people to become more interested in celebrating it. The final decision took decades to reach – various proposals had been bandied about under a succession of governments.

There are also groups lobbying for the introduction of an official National Pastry, and a National Dish, and for the key-fiddle (*nyckelharpa*) to be made the National Instrument. But even for ideas as innocent as these, arriving at a consensus has proved difficult.

*The Royal Family always takes part in the National Day festivities.*

## National Day

Since 1983, Sweden has celebrated its National Day on 6 June. This is the date on which Gustav Vasa was crowned king in 1523 and on which a new constitution was adopted in 1809. The original idea came from Artur Hazelius, who founded the Skansen open-air museum in Stockholm and held a national day celebration there on 6 June as early as the 1890s. At the 1893 World Fair in Chicago, Sweden presented Midsummer Day as a form of Swedish national day, and it was subsequently proposed that this arrangement be officially sanctioned at home. As Hazelius organised Skansen's national day festivity at the end of spring, Sweden celebrated the occasion twice a year in the 1890s. In 1916, Hazelius's idea was officially adopted and 6 June became Swedish Flag Day. The name celebrated the fact that Sweden had acquired its own flag following the dissolution of the union with Norway in 1905.

# Midsummer

**SUMMER IN SWEDEN** is short. It starts showing its face in May and explodes into life in June. The summer has to hurry to get things done before the nights turn cold in September and everything stops growing. At Midsummer, the Swedish summer is a lush green and bursting with chlorophyll, and the nights are scarcely dark at all. In the north, the sun never sets.

Swedes are fairly well attuned to the rhythms of nature. At Midsummer, many begin their five-week annual holidays and they, too, are in a hurry to get things done. Midsummer Eve is celebrated in the countryside – as always – and on the day before,

everyone leaves town, everything closes and the streets are suddenly spookily deserted.

The country's main thoroughfares, on the other hand, are packed. Queues of cars stretch away into the distance, and at the end of the road, family and friends wait among silver birches in full, shimmering bloom. Midsummer is an occasion of large gatherings – and to be honest, many Swedes take advantage of it to fulfil their social obligations so that they can enjoy the rest of their holiday in peace. In many cases, whole families gather to celebrate this traditional high-point of the summer.

Swedes like the world to be well-ordered, so

*Ring dance round the flower-bedecked maypole – a typical Midsummer activity.*

Midsummer Eve is always a Friday. People often begin the day by picking flowers and making wreaths to place on the maypole, which is a key component in the celebrations. The maypole is raised in an open spot and traditional ring-dances ensue, to the delight of the children and some of the adults. Teenagers tend to stay out of it and wait for the evening's more riotous entertainment.

A typical Midsummer menu features different kinds of pickled herring, boiled new potatoes with fresh dill, soured cream and chives. This is often followed by a grilled dish of some kind, such as spare rib or salmon, and for dessert the first strawberries of summer, with cream. The traditional accompaniment is a cold beer and schnapps, preferably spiced. Every time the glasses are refilled, singing breaks out anew. Swedes like drinking-songs, and the racier the better.

Midsummer is an occasion invested with a certain nostalgia. Deep inside, Swedes are all agreed on what it should look like and how it should proceed. So after dinner, many people still want to go out dancing, just like in the old days. Preferably on an outdoor dance floor beside a lake as the evening mist settles and the sound of the orchestra echoes back from the rocky hills on the opposite shore.

On their way home, girls and young women are supposed to pick seven different species of flowers and lay them under their pillows. At night, their future husbands appear to them in a dream.

Legend has it that the night before Midsummer's Day is a magical time for love. It still is, in a way. During the longest night of the year, many a relationship is put to the test. Under the influence of alcohol, the truth will out, which can lead both to marriage and to divorce. Like Whitsun, Midsummer is a popular time of year for weddings and christening ceremonies. Despite their poor showing as churchgoers, Swedes still like to wed in a country church with a flower-bedecked, arched entrance and beautiful hymns.

*Traditional foods are at the heart of Midsummer celebrations.*

*A refreshing dip in the light Midsummer night.*

## Midsummer

Midsummer Day was originally celebrated on 24 June to commemorate John the Baptist. In 1953, it was moved to the nearest Saturday.

In agrarian times, Midsummer celebrations in Sweden were held to welcome summertime and the season of fertility. In some areas, therefore, people dressed up as 'green men', clad in ferns. They also decorated their houses and farm tools with foliage, and raised tall, leafy maypoles to dance around, probably as early as the 16th century and modelled on a German tradition. Midsummer was primarily an occasion for young people, but it was also celebrated in the industrial communities of central Sweden, where all mill employees were given a feast

of pickled herring, beer and schnapps. It was not until the 20th century, however, that this became the most Swedish of all traditional festivities.

Ever since the 6th century AD, Midsummer bonfires have been lit around Europe. In Sweden, they were mainly found in the southern part of the country. Young people also liked to visit holy springs, where they drank the healing waters and amused themselves with games and dancing. These visits were a reminder of how John the Baptist baptised Christ in the River Jordan.

Midsummer Night is the lightest of the year and was long considered a magical night, as it was the best time for telling people's futures. Girls ate

salted porridge ('dream porridge') so that their future husbands might bring water to them in their dreams, to quench their thirst. They also kept watch at springs for a reflection of their husband-to-be in the water.

On Midsummer Night, you could discover places where treasure was buried, for example by studying how moonbeams fell. When digging, you might be confronted by strange sights that would tempt you to laugh or speak, such as a lame hen pulling a large hay-load. If you managed to keep quiet, you would find the treasure.

Also that night, it was said, water was turned into wine and ferns into flowers. Many plants acquired healing powers on that one night of the year.

# The crayfish party

**AS THE SWEDISH** summer draws to a close, you may be lucky enough to experience warm, clear August nights that are almost Mediterranean in character. That's when Swedes have their crayfish parties.

Due to the risk of over-fishing, restrictions on river crayfishing were introduced back in the early 20th century. The season was limited to a couple of months from August. Crayfish thus became an exclusive and much sought-after delicacy. The crayfish population has also been decimated on a number of occasions by a dreaded parasitic mould.

Today, imported crayfish are on sale all year round, but few Swedes are prepared to abandon the seasonal tradition. In early August, the media set the scene for the feast with detailed tests of the current year's offerings, tips from celebrities and lists ranking the various brands. In some years, Chinese crayfish are deemed best, in others those imported from the US. But Swedish crayfish – needless to say – are always adjudged the best. The trouble is, they are very expensive. Whatever their origin, crayfish in Sweden are cooked as the Swedes like them – in a brine, with plenty of crown dill.

The very few who have private access, of course, catch their own crayfish. The little creatures are night animals, so fishing has to be done after dark. They are caught in wire traps and the bait is often

*Both crayfishing and crayfish parties are a play between light and dark.*

## The crayfish feast

Crayfish have been eaten in Sweden since the 16th century. For a long while, only the aristocracy partook of these delicacies, as popular suspicion of shellfish was widespread. Originally, crayfish meat was used for sausage, ragout, patties or puddings.

In the mid-19th century, people started eating crayfish as they are eaten today. The crayfish feast or crayfish supper in the month of August spread through the middle classes.

In the 20th century, crayfish became a national delicacy and people in all sectors of society began celebrating the occasion. The price of crayfish fell as a result of imports from Turkey and elsewhere. The crayfish feast, at which people gather to eat, drink and be merry, is a typically Swedish festivity marking the end of the summer.

rotten or raw fish. Crayfish must be alive when placed in the saucepan of boiling liquor.

Once a preserve of the moneyed classes, the crayfish party is today an occasion for all. Over the years, certain aspects of it have become a tradition. Crayfish are to be eaten outdoors, and gaily coloured paper lanterns should be hung round the table. The most popular type of lantern shows a smiling full moon. Both the tablecloth and the colourful plates are also supposed to be of paper. People wear bibs round their necks and comic paper hats on their heads. Then the feast begins. You eat crayfish cold, with your fingers. Sucking noisily to extract the juices is perfectly acceptable behaviour. Bread and a strong cheese such as mature Västerbotten are eaten on the side. People mostly drink beer and the inevitable schnapps.

# The Surströmming premiere

**ALL COUNTRIES HAVE** their own dreaded delicacies – insects, strange entrails and pieces of meat in various stages of decay. Sweden has the notorious sour herring (*surströmming*). Not all Swedes eat it, but the dish has become increasingly popular, even among gourmets. While sour herring is a Swedish tradition, it is also fair to say that those who eat it do so because they like the taste. No-one eats it for fun.

The dish is made from the small Baltic herring, which is caught in the spring, salted and 'soured' (fermented) according to a time-honoured process. About a month before it is due on the table, it is packed in hermetically sealed tins, but fermenta-

*You are advised to open sour herring tins outdoors!*

tion continues, and in time the tins swell, both on top and underneath. By tradition, most producers are to be found along the coast of northern Sweden.

As considerable pressure has built up in the tin, it should be opened under water. You then wash the herring before serving it. The tin should be opened outdoors but its contents are best eaten indoors as the smell attracts flies.

Sour herring has a strong, pungent smell of rotting fish. Enthusiasts love this smell while new-comers reel back in shock. But a well-prepared fermented herring doesn't taste the way it smells. On the contrary. The taste is simultaneously rounded and sharp, spicy and savoury. Accoutrements are needed, however, to maintain a balance.

The traditional way of eating sour herring is wrapped in a 'thin-bread' sandwich (*klämma*). You butter the bread, place the gutted herring on it together with slices of almond-shaped potato (*mandelpotatis*) and chopped onion, fold it up and eat it with your hands. The slight sweetness of the potato and onion offsets the sharp, intense taste of the fish perfectly. In northern areas, people butter their bread with soft whey-cheese made from goat's milk (*getmessmör*), as well as with ordinary butter.

The sour herring premiere takes place at the end of August, when the spring catch comes onto the market. True enthusiasts, however, eat the previous year's vintage. By that time, the herring is fully matured and tender.

### The Surströmming premiere

*Surströmming* – fermented Baltic herring – is produced by means of an ancient souring method used in Northern Europe and Asia for preserving fish. In the old days, the dish was everyday fare for the peasants of northern Sweden, and was often taken along as provisions by hunters or travellers. Today, it is more seasonal in character. Eating this strong-smelling delicacy is something of a test of man-hood, and the dish tends to divide the population into two camps – those for and those against.

# Halloween

**THE CELEBRATION OF** a particular custom often has lengthy roots. Some customs are traditional, with the emphasis on their religious origins, while others are of a contemporary, more commercial nature. When a custom is exported, however, the roots are usually cut. So Halloween pumpkins in Sweden are made of plastic and the children's fancy-dress costumes were bought at the supermarket round the corner.

Halloween has only been celebrated in Sweden since the 1990s, and has rapidly become established here – not least as a result of smart commercial marketing. By the beginning of November, Sweden is enveloped in darkness and the long working weeks stretch away endlessly. There are no public holidays or extended weekends in the calendar between the summer holiday and All Saints' Day. Halloween heralds the schools' autumn break and represents a welcome diversion in the gathering dark.

The occasion is mainly celebrated by children and teenagers. They go to fancy-dress parties and ghost parties, light lanterns and venture forth into the streets to scare the life out of the neighbourhood.

Many pubs and restaurants stage Halloween parties and decorate their premises with fearsome attributes. Halloween has come to stay.

On the island of Öland in the southern Baltic, the arrival of Halloween has led to an upswing in pumpkin growing, and the giant fruits are now quite readily available.

*The idea is to look as scary as possible!*

## Halloween

With the rise of Christianity, the heathen Samhain came to be called Hallowmas, or All Saints' Day, to commemorate the souls of the dead who had been canonised that year, so the night before became popularly known as Halloween, All Hallows Eve. Samhain was a Celtic harvest festival marking the end of summer and the beginning of winter labours. That night was regarded as a magical time of transition, when the dead called on the living and various supernatural creatures were a foot. People lit fires, dressed up and went round begging from door to door (trick-or-treat). They carved faces in turnips and lit them inside with candles. These glowing vegetables were supposed to represent the wandering soul of Jack the Blacksmith and were called Jack O'Lanterns.

Halloween was imported into the US by Irish immigrants in the 1840s and became a popular festivity there. The pumpkin replaced the turnip and the occasion was celebrated with trick-or-treat and special parades. In the 1990s, Halloween became established in Sweden, where it is mainly celebrated in macabre fashion by children and young people.

# All Saints' Day

**ALL SAINTS' DAY** is a day of dignity and reflection. The custom of lighting candles on family graves is still widely practised, and anyone travelling through Sweden on this weekend is met by some beautiful scenes. With luck, the first snow has fallen over the country's cemeteries. The countless points of light from the candles and lanterns placed on graves form beautiful patterns in the snow and lend a special feel to the landscape.

People also lay flowers and wreaths on graves on All Saints' Day. A jar of flowering heather stands up well to the cold.

In southern Sweden, outdoor work is nearing completion, while in the north, All Saints' Day marks the first day of winter and the traditional start of the alpine ski season.

Until recently, shops and stores were closed to mark the occasion. Although this is no longer the case everywhere, most Swedes take the day off, and those who don't visit cemeteries usually stay at home with the family and cook an ambitious meal of some kind. Many churches organise concerts to celebrate All Saints' Day.

## All Saints' Day

In AD 731, 1 November was designated a day of remembrance for saints of the church who had no days of their own. From the 11th century, 2 November was dedicated to all the dead, of whatever standing, and was called All Souls' Day. It was widely observed by the populace, with requiems and bell-ringing, but was abolished with the arrival of the Reformation. In 1772, All Saints' Day was moved to the first Sunday in November and in 1953 to the Saturday between 31 October and 6 November.

In olden days, graves were decorated at Christmastime, when small candle-lit Christmas trees were placed on the graves of young children. In the 20th century, however, people began putting lighted candles on the graves of the departed on All Saints' Day. This custom originated with wealthy families in towns and cities. But after the Second World War, it spread throughout the country, beginning in the Stockholm region. Churches also began holding services of light to mark the day.

*Candles are lit as dusk gathers across the country's graveyards.*

# St Martin's Day or 'Martin goose'

**ST MARTIN'S DAY** is a celebration of the goose – all other connotations have largely been forgotten. In early November, geese are ready for slaughter, and on 11 November it is time for the traditional dinner of roast goose. Some people cook the dish themselves but the majority go out to a restaurant. The custom is particularly popular in Skåne in southern Sweden, where goose farming has long been practised, but it has gradually spread northwards.

A goose dinner is something of a banquet. It takes time to cook and is very filling. All parts of the goose are used. The dinner begins with a bowl of sweet and sour 'black soup' (*svartsoppa*), made from goose blood and goose broth, and richly seasoned with fruit pureés, spirits and spices such as clove and ginger. The soup is thick and reddish black in colour.

Black soup is served with entrails of various kinds, as well as goose-liver sausage, stewed prunes and potatoes.

The goose is stuffed with apples and prunes and roasted slowly while being constantly basted in its own fat. The carcass is then boiled in water, which is thickened into sauce. The surplus fat is used to prepare the trimmings: red cabbage, roasted apples and potatoes. As if this weren't enough, a proper goose dinner also includes apple charlotte.

*Delicious also with apple and prune stuffing – not to mention black soup.*

## St Martin's Day ('Martin Goose')

St Martin of Tours originally took the goose as his personal symbol, because when trying to avoid being ordained bishop he had hidden in a goose pen, where he was betrayed by the cackling of the geese. He celebrates his nameday in November, when the geese are ready for killing. St Martin's Day was an important medieval autumn feast, and the custom of eating goose spread to Sweden from France. It was primarily observed by the craftsmen and noblemen of the towns. In the peasant community, however, not everyone could afford to eat goose, so many ate duck or hen instead.

Today, people mostly eat goose in the southernmost province of Skåne and in university towns. Before, it was eaten in the Stockholm region as well. The practice of eating 'black soup' and goose in the same meal is relatively new and probably has its roots in the catering world.

St Martin's was also an important day for those who believed in chance. If it snowed that day there would be no snow at Christmas. If the holiday coincided with a Friday or Saturday, the coming winter would be harsh.

# Advent

**BY THE TIME DECEMBER** comes round, Sweden has very few hours of daylight. The sun drops out of sight in the afternoon. The first Sunday of Advent comes as an eagerly awaited sign that Christmas is approaching. Although by then, of course, the world of commerce has made sure we know what is coming – sales campaigns begin in mid-November and Christmas shop windows and street decorations are already in place.

While the commercial decorations are there for a specific purpose, they also have a wider effect – they keep the dark at bay. Throughout the country, Swedes help by putting electrical candlesticks in their windows – sometimes one in each – and arranging lights on a Christmas tree in the garden. In northern Sweden, where the midnight sun shines in the summer, the sun never rises above the horizon at this time of year. "It'll soon turn", Swedes tell one another when they meet. The midwinter solstice, on 21 December, is just round the corner, and the days will then begin to get lighter.

On the first Sunday, people light the first candle in the Advent candlestick. This is always a special event, eagerly awaited. Each Sunday until Christmas, a candle is lit (and blown out after a while), until all four candles are alight. The children's expectations grow with every candle. On TV, there is a special Christmas calendar show for the young

*Ginger snaps and toffee need to be ready in time.*
*And the Advent candlesticks with four candles –*
*one for each Sunday – are prominently displayed.*
*When all are lit, Christmas is at hand.*

# Advent

Advent means arrival, or coming, and since the 5th century AD has heralded the Christmas season and the birth of Christ. Since the 1890s, the custom in Sweden has been to light a candle every Sunday during Advent. The candles used to be placed in tiny Christmas trees, but from the 1930s onwards these were superseded by candlesticks of iron or wood. The Moravian custom of hanging a star made from paper, straw or chipwood in windows also found its way to Sweden in the 1930s, recalling the star that guided the Three Wise Men. The advent calendar dates from around this time as well. Children open a window in the calendar for each passing day until Christmas Eve.

In agrarian times, Advent was a hectic period when all farmwork was to be completed so that people could take Christmas leave. By 9 December, 'Anna Day', the Christmas brew was to be ready, the lutfisk was to be soaked in lye and the baking was to begin. On Lucia Day, 13 December, candles were to be made and animals slaughtered for the Christmas table, and after Tomas Day, 21 December, all milling and spinning was to cease. Christmas fairs were then held in town. Since the Middle Ages, Swedes have drunk hot mulled wine (*glögg*), during Advent.

with 24 episodes. It, too, serves as a countdown to the big day.

In towns and cities, Christmas fairs selling handicrafts and decorations are a common sight, while at home people start baking in preparation for the holiday.

December is one of the most hectic months for Swedish families. The burden of work is always heavy at this time of year. There is much to be done in a short space of time before everyone can sit back and relax. For the children, meanwhile, December involves numerous end-of-term ceremonies, shows and activities. The longed-for peace and quiet comes later, when all the preparations have been completed and Christmas can begin in earnest.

On the first Sunday in Advent, many Swedes get together to drink *glögg* – a hot, spicy mulled wine with blanched almonds and raisins and ginger snaps to accompany it.

# Lucia

**SWEDEN IS AN EGALITARIAN** place these days, so any child can be chosen as Lucia for the annual procession at the local daycare centre, not just pretty ones with long blonde hair. The boys usually prefer to be brownies (*tomtar*) or 'star boys' (*stjärngossar*) in the procession, while quite a few girls agree to be Lucia's handmaidens (*tärnor*). The real candles once used are now battery-powered, but there is still a special atmosphere when the lights are dimmed and the sound of the children singing grows as they enter from an adjacent room. Tradition has it that Lucia is to wear 'light in her hair', which in practice means a crown of electric candles in a wreath on her head. Each of her handmaidens carries a candle, too. Parents gather in the dark with their mobile cameras at the ready.

The star boys, who like the handmaidens are dressed in white gowns, carry stars on sticks and have tall paper cones on their heads. The brownies bring up the rear, carrying small lanterns.

Competition for the role of Lucia can be tough. Each year, a national Lucia is proclaimed in one or other of the TV channels, while every town and village worth the name chooses its own Lucia. Candidates are presented in the local newspaper a couple of weeks in advance. Staunchly opposed

*Saffron buns (lussebullar) och hot mulled wine (glögg) are a 'must' on Lucia Day.*

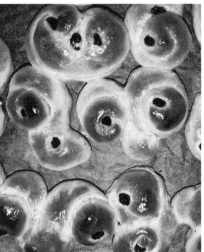

*On Lucia Day, parents get the chance to try out their new mobile cameras.*

to privilege, Sweden has always sought to avoid ranking people, which is why beauty contests and 'homecoming queen' events are rare. The Lucia celebration, however, has been an exception. Every year, local newspaper subscribers are invited to vote for one or other of the candidates. You can no longer count on the blonde winning, although many a Miss Sweden has started out as the local Lucia. On Lucia Day, the winner is announced and is then driven around town, preferably in a horse-drawn vehicle of some kind, to spread light and song in food stores, factories, old-age homes and medical centres.

Alongside Midsummer, the Lucia celebrations represent one of the foremost cultural traditions in Sweden, with their clear reference to life in the peasant communities of old: darkness and light, cold and warmth.

Lucia is an ancient mythical figure with an abiding role as a bearer of light in the dark Swedish winters.

The many Lucia songs all have the same theme:

*The night treads heavily*
*around yards and dwellings*
*In places unreached by sun,*
*the shadows brood*
*Into our dark house she comes,*
*bearing lighted candles,*
*Saint Lucia, Saint Lucia.*

All Swedes know the standard Lucia song by heart, and everyone can sing it, in or out of tune. On the morning of Lucia Day, the radio plays some rather more expert renderings, by school choirs or the like. The Lucia celebrations also include ginger snaps and sweet, saffronflavoured buns (*lussekatter*) shaped like curled-up cats and with raisin eyes. You eat them with *glögg* or coffee.

## Lucia, 13 December

The Lucia tradition can be traced back both to St Lucia of Syracuse, a martyr who died in 304, and to the Swedish legend of Lucia as Adam's first wife. It is said that she consorted with the Devil and that her children were invisible infernals. Thus the name may be associated with both lux (light) and Lucifer (Satan), and its origins are difficult to determine. The present custom appears to be a blend of traditions.

In the old almanac, Lucia Night was the longest of the year. It was a dangerous night when supernatural beings were abroad and all animals could speak. By morning, when they were said to have bitten the manger three times out of hunger, the livestock needed extra feed. People, too, needed extra nourishment and were urged to eat seven or nine hearty breakfasts. This kind of feasting presaged the Christmas fast, which began on Lucia Day.

The last person to rise that morning was nicknamed 'Lusse the Louse' and often given a playful beating round the legs with birch twigs. The slaughtering and threshing were supposed to be over by Lucia and the sheds to be filled with food in preparation for Christmas. In agrarian Sweden, young people used to dress up as Lucia figures (*lussegubbar*) that night and wander from house to house singing songs and scrounging for food and schnapps.

The first recorded appearance of a white-clad Lucia in Sweden was in a country house in 1764. The custom did not become universally popular in Swedish society until the 20th century, when schools and local associations in particular began promoting it. The old *lussegubbar* custom virtually disappeared with urban migration, and white-clad Lucias with their singing processions were considered a more acceptable, controlled form of celebration than the youthful carousals of the past. Stockholm proclaimed its first Lucia in 1927. The custom whereby Lucia serves coffee and buns (*lussekatter*) dates back to the 1880s, although the buns were around long before that.

# Christmas

**AFTER NEARLY A MONTH** of waiting, Christmas Eve finally arrives – the height of the celebration in Sweden. Work is at an end, schoolchildren are on holiday and the Christmas preparations are complete. People have bought their presents and their Christmas food in crowded shops and department stores, and the home has been cleaned and decorated according to each family's traditional habits.

Christmas is the main family event of the year, and there is always a certain amount of discussion about where to celebrate it this time round. Sweden, as we have mentioned, is a large country, and those wishing to be reunited with their families often have to travel far. Train and air tickets need be booked at least two months in advance, and motorists are advised to start their journeys in good time.

Christmas in Sweden is a blend of domestic and foreign customs that have been re-interpreted, refined and commercialised on their way from agrarian society to the modern age. Today, most Swedes celebrate Christmas in roughly the same way, and many of the local customs and specialities have disappeared, although each family claims to celebrate it in true fashion in their own particular way.

The food you eat at Christmas may still depend on where you live in the country, or where you

*Waiting for Santa Claus can take all day. At least that's how it seems to many children.*

came from originally. But here, too, homogenisation has set in, due in no small part to the uniform offerings of the department stores and the ready availability of convenience foods. Few have time to salt their own hams or stuff their own pork sausages nowadays.

Ingmar Bergman's Oscar-winning film 'Fanny and Alexander', although set in the late 19th century, nevertheless reflects Swedish Christmas celebrations today: a bright and lively occasion, full of excess, good food and happiness, but also a time during which family secrets tend to surface.

Holiday leave over Christmas and the New Year is fairly long, usually extending a week into January. Once Christmas Eve is over, a series of enjoyable – or, in some cases, dutiful – visits to friends and relatives ensues. Swedes travel many a mile during the holiday period. Christmas Day with the Olssons, Boxing Day with the Perssons and a week's skiing in the mountains with the Svenssons.

Perhaps celebrating Christmas is more complicated than ever nowadays. Present-day family constellations, comprising ex-wives and ex-husbands, children from marriages old and new, newly-acquired relatives and mothers-in-law, are

all hard to fit into the nuclear family celebration that, deep down, all Swedes prefer. As though they weren't already under enough pressure to celebrate a perfect Christmas.

As a rule, Swedes expect a great deal from their Christmases. There should be snow on the ground but blue skies and sunshine, everyone is expected to be in good health, the ham must be succulent and tasty, and presents must be numerous. Moreover, the children are expected to be happy and well-behaved and the home is expected to be warm and bright.

Everyone does their best, and the Swedes perhaps are better placed than most to celebrate Christmas. The ever-present candles and lights provide a nice contrast to the winter dark, the red wooden cottages are at their most attractive when embedded in snow, and the fir trees stand dark and sedate at the edge of the forest. Santa Claus moves about the land and the North Star pulsates up there in the night sky.

On the day before Christmas Eve, Swedes venture forth to look for the perfect Christmas tree. This is a serious matter – the tree is the very symbol of Christmas, and it must be densely and evenly branched, and straight. If you live in a city or town, you buy the tree in the street or square. Those who live in the country fell their Christmas trees themselves. Many Swedes believe – mistakenly – that their legal right of access to the countryside allows them to fetch a tree from the woods wherever they like, with an axe, a bucksaw or – as in western Värmland on the Norwegian border – with a shotgun. Not to be recommended.

Trees are decorated according to family tradition. Some are bedecked with flags, others with tinsel and many with coloured baubles. Electric lights are usually preferred to candles on the tree because of the risk of fire. Homes are also decorated with wall hangings depicting brownies and winter scenes, with tablecloths in Christmas patterns, and with candlesticks, little Father Christmas figures and angels. The home is filled with the powerful scent of hyacinths.

At 3 p.m., the whole of Sweden turns on the TV to watch a cavalcade of Disney film scenes that have been shown ever since the 1960s without anyone tiring of them. Only then can the celebrations begin in earnest.

Christmas presents are under the lighted tree, candles shine brightly and the smörgåsbord has been prepared with all the classic dishes: Christmas ham, pork sausage, an egg and anchovy mixture (*gubbröra*), herring salad, pickled herring, home-made liver patty, wort-flavoured rye bread (*vörtbröd*), potatoes and a special fish dish, *lutfisk*. The ham is first boiled, then painted and glazed with a mixture of egg, breadcrumbs and mustard. Lutfisk is dried ling or sathe soaked in water and lye before it is cooked.

Once all have eaten their fill, Santa Claus himself arrives to wish the gathering a Merry Christmas and distribute the presents.

with wall hangings, and fresh straw was laid on floors. The birds were given an oatsheaf and the mythical farm-yard brownie a plate of porridge. The practice of bringing a Christmas tree into the house and decorating it was imported from Germany in the 1880s. Initially, Christmas presents were given anonymously, and playfully, often in the form of a log of wood or the like wrapped up and tossed through a front door. In the 20th century, people began giving one another real presents, handed out by Santa Claus, who was modelled on St. Nicholas, the patron saint of school-children.

At the early-morning church service (*julotta*) on Christmas Day, traces of earth could be seen in the pews where the dead had held their own service overnight. After the service, people raced to get home first. The winner would harvest his crops before anyone else that year.

On Boxing Day, you got up early to water the horses in streams running north, as Saint Stephen (Staffan), the patron saint of horses, was said to have done. Another practice, which breached the no-work rule, was to muck out other people's barns.

Twelfth Night commemorates the arrival of the Three Wise Men in Bethlehem. The Swedish tradition of 'star boys' (*stjärngossar*) derives from this. In former times, boys often went round the farms carrying a paper star, singing songs in return for schnapps. Today, the star boys are a part of the Lucia celebration.

Hilarymas (*Knutsdagen*) on 13 Janu-ary marked the end of the Christmas holiday in Sweden, and was celebrated with a final medieval-style feast. People scared one another with straw figures hung from trees. In bourgeois circles, the Christmas tree was plundered of its edible decorations. Tree-plundering is still practised in Sweden today.

## Christmas

Christmas, which commemorates the birth of Christ, has long been the most important festivity of the year. In the old days, it was a feast for the whole household as there was plenty of fresh food to be had. The Christmas table was laid with ham, pickled herring, jellied pig's feet, sausage, rice porridge and *lutfisk* (ling). The food was to be left on the table overnight, as it was then that the dead came to feast.

Homes were cleaned and decorated